The Story of
Toilets, Telephones
& other useful inventions

Katie Daynes

Illustrated by
Adam Larkum

Reading Consultant: Alison Kelly
University of Surrey Roehampton

Contents

Chapter 1

The story of toilets

Long ago, people didn't even have houses, so building a toilet was the last thing on their minds.

Then they learned to farm
the land and made themselves
homes to live in.

Some built a toilet in the
yard, but it was only a hole in
the ground. When the hole
filled up, they simply covered
it with mud and dug another.
This worked fine... until they
ran out of space.

The ancient Romans had a much better idea – public toilets. They placed a long, stone slab with holes over a deep trench. Then they decorated the toilet room with marble and mosaics.

Going to the toilet became a great way to meet people. Romans sat in a row, chatting about politics and plays. Below them, water flowed through the trench and washed everything away.

At Roman banquets, rich guests didn't even have to leave the room. They simply asked a slave to bring in a silver pot and filled it there and then.

In later times, people were more shy about these things. Lords and ladies preferred to go alone, using fancy, cushioned toilet boxes, often hidden behind a curtain.

These were a lot more comfortable – though someone then had to empty them.

Castles and fortresses had
basic toilets built into their
design. Some jutted out from
the main building,
emptying onto
the moat below.

Yuck!

Stinky moats were great
protection. No enemy wanted
to wade through them.

10

But the smells were about to get worse. Medieval towns were being built and everyone had forgotten the Roman public toilets. Luckily, they still had pots.

These allowed people to go in the comfort of their own bedroom. They were known as chamber pots.

But the pots had to be emptied and the easiest way was out of a window.

Unlucky passers-by got a yucky surprise. With nowhere for the waste to drain away, the smell on the streets was disgusting. It's a wonder anyone ever went shopping.

12

Kings and queens had to introduce toilet laws.

"I forbid you from dumping filth in rivers or on streets," Edward III announced to the people of London.

Where else can it go?

The problem was finally solved by laying pipes and drains underground. Toilet filth could now glide away *under* the street, not over it.

Of course, when something got stuck, the mess was awful.

In 1596, Sir John Harington, godson of Queen Elizabeth I, had a brainwave. "I'll invent a toilet that flushes!"

A royal flush!

Making the flush work properly took ages. In fact, most people didn't have a flush for another 200 years.

Many plumbers worked hard to improve toilet designs, including a man named Thomas Crapper. He set up his own Crapper plumbing shops in London and took charge of the royal toilets.

By 1880, the toilet had really arrived. Since then, only the shapes and decorations have changed.

Some are fitted into the wall...

...others are made to look like thrones.

Space toilets even have bars to stop you from floating away.

16

Today, we take toilets for granted. But spend a day in the woods and you'll soon learn how things were for our ancestors.

Chapter 2

Telephones

Alexander Graham Bell was a boy with a mission. While his father taught deaf people how to talk, Alexander wanted to find out how words travel.

His mother was deaf, but young Alexander found a way to make her hear. If he talked with his lips pressed against her forehead, she could feel his words and understand him.

When Bell grew up, he got a job teaching deaf people to speak. In his spare time, he loved to experiment with sound.

One day, he played a chord on a piano and heard the exact notes echo on a piano next door.

"The notes can travel through air," he realized. His mind buzzed with ideas. If all sounds could travel, perhaps he could send speech from one place to another.

Wouldn't that be amazing!

21

In those days, 150 years ago, the quickest way to send messages over long distances was by telegraph. A message was tapped at one end of an electric wire...

dot dot dash dot dash dash dot dot dot dash dash dash dot dot

...and finally received at the other.

The tapping code had been invented by an American professor, Samuel Morse. But changing messages in and out of code took forever.

Bell thought long and hard about telegraph wires and speech. One day, he jumped up in excitement.

"I'll turn speech into an electric current," he thought. "Then it can travel down the telegraph wires."

In 1876, with the help of Thomas Watson, an electrical engineer, he invented a mouthpiece and an earpiece. They looked exactly the same and were joined together by an electric wire.

"When I speak into the mouthpiece, a metal flap will move," said Bell, "and my words will travel down the wire as an electric current."

"Then the flap on the earpiece will move," added Watson, "and I'll be able to hear you!"

They quickly put their theory to the test. Watson sat alone, holding the earpiece... Suddenly, Bell's voice boomed out.

Mr. Watson, come here. I want to see you.

And so the life of the phone began. In 1877, Bell set off through North America and Europe to promote his new invention.

"How modern!" thought Queen Victoria, immediately ordering one for her palace.

Tell John Brown to saddle up the horses.

The first phones needed
operators to connect people.
  "Number please," said an
operator, when someone lifted
a receiver. Once the operator
had linked two telephone lines
together, a conversation
could begin.

28

By the late 1890s, automatic switchboards had been invented and lots of operators were out of a job. Within ten years, everyone wanted a phone.

Early phones had a handle you turned as you listened.

Then there
were boxes
that people
spoke into...

a speaker
shaped like a
candlestick...

and the
cradle phone.

Today, millions of people own mobiles. A phone with no wire would have really impressed Alexander Bell – especially one that can send pictures too.

Chapter 3

Frozen food

It was 1913 and an American named Clarence Birdseye was trading fur in northern Canada. "How can anyone live in this icy place?" he wondered.

A local man offered to show him around. Dressed in a thick fur coat, Birdseye joined a huddle of fishermen around three holes in the ice. Everyone was dangling a line into the chilly water.

This isn't my idea of fun.

With a sudden tug, one of the men yanked out a fish. It flipped in the air and froze, before landing on the ice with a clunk.

"Is that tonight's supper?" asked Birdseye.

"No way," replied the fisherman. "We've already got enough fish to last a month!"

Birdseye was amazed. Where he came from, fish went rotten and smelly within a day. Did frozen fish really keep fresh? That evening at supper he tasted the answer.

Birdseye's brain started working overtime. "At home, people would pay good money for frozen food!" he thought.

Back in America, he invented a quick freeze machine and started the world's first frozen food company – Birds Eye.

Chapter 4

Soccer nets

John Brodie was crazy about soccer. Every Saturday he sat in the stadium cheering as his team won, lost or drew.

At one match, Brodie and his friends watched their top striker kick the ball between the goal posts.

"Hooray!" they cheered, but the referee shook his head. He didn't think a goal had been scored.

For the rest of the match,
Brodie sat sulking. Then he
had an idea. "I'll design a net
to go behind the posts,"
he thought. "It will
trap the ball
and prove there's
been a goal."

Chapter 5

Safety razors

King Camp Gillette was trying to shave on a steam train. Despite his grand name, he was only a salesman going to a meeting.

As the train jerked forward, he cut his chin.

"Ow!" he cried, looking at a drop of blood on his cut-throat razor. "There must be a safer way to shave..."

At the meeting, Gillette sat dabbing his chin with a blood-spotted handkerchief.

The company president was making a long, boring speech. "Toothbrushes are big business because they always need replacing," he said. "We must sell more products that wear out quickly."

Years later, Gillette stood in front of his mirror, making a face. He'd bought a new kind of razor, but already the blade was blunt.

"I spend my life sharpening blades," he thought.

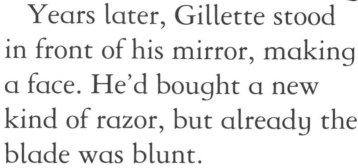

Then it came to him – the invention that would change his life.

"I'll make a razor with a safe, removable blade!" he cried. "When it goes blunt, you can throw it away and buy another. No one will bother sharpening any more – they'll just keep coming back for new blades!"

This is the future of shaving.

And they did.

45

Other useful inventions

Before the **wheel** was invented, 5,500 years ago, carrying things and going places took ages.

If it wasn't for Stanislau Baudry, we'd still be waiting for the bus. He started the first **bus service** in 1827 to take people to his baths outside Paris.

Until 1850, no one had a **refrigerator**. Without fridges today, the food we keep would smell awful.

In 1938, Ladislao Biro was fed up with ink pens that smudged. So, he invented a pen with quick drying ink and called it a...

46

When people started exploring space, it led to even more exciting inventions.

Have you noticed **bar codes** at supermarkets? They were first used to label the millions of parts that make up a spacecraft.

The material used in **firefighters' suits** and the flexible folds on **ski boots** were originally designed for astronauts.

The first **smoke detector** was made for a space station. Now most homes have one too.

47

Series editor: Lesley Sims

Designed by
Russell Punter and Natacha Goransky

Goal net advice:
National Museum of Football

First published in 2004 by Usborne Publishing Ltd., Usborne House,
83-85 Saffron Hill, London EC1N 8RT, England. www.usborne.com
Copyright © 2004 Usborne Publishing Ltd.